Lagos Is Killing Me

Oloyede Michael Taiwo

First published in Great Britain as a
softback original in 2021

Editing and Proofreading
Hungry Bookstore

Cover Design: Buzz Designs

Published by 'The Roaring Lion Newcastle'
ISBN: 978-1-913636-98-2

Email:
books@theroaringlionnewcastle.com

Website:
www.theroaringlionnewcastle.com

THE ROARING LION
NEWCASTLE LTD

DEDICATION

This book is dedicated to God Almighty and the wind beneath my wings, my mother, Sadetu Lawal Oloyede and to the blessed memory of my father, Segun Oloyede.

Table of Contents

ACKNOWLEDGEMENTS

To all the gracious palms that have spent time and effort, counsel and widows' mites to mould this nostalgic clay of words into reality, thank you, I am so grateful.

And to my twin sister, Kehinde Oloyede Ajayi and her kids, Ore ofe and Wisdom; my big sister, Seun Oloyede and her son, Iyanuoluwa. I love you.

Special thanks to Tobi Adeyemi, a friend that sticks closer than a brother, for his restless effort and continual dedication to my progress. And for both your piercing and soothing words; I love you.

Special thanks to Dare and Ireti Adeyemi and their brilliant children. You all are so gracious and special in all dimensions.

I will like to thank everyone in my path who has had my back at certain points in time: Sunday Alabi, Odunjo Gbenga (Apex Academy), Dare Fadun, Dipo Akinrinlade, Itunu Olofinjana, Seun Oloyede, Goke Fatogun, Kazeem Adigun, Otor Mathew, Efe Paul Azino, Sage Hasson, Titi Oyemade, Ileri, Souzan Koku David, Opeoluwa Ogunbiyi, Tunde Opaleye, Jimi Ilori, Osagie Aigbogun, Michael Bossomo, Anthony Ebadan, ID Cabasa, Alaba Abimbola, Obizulike Chukwuma (Narrator), Seni Osifala, Taiwo Sonaike (Talaranta), Yomi Abdul Olugbode, Emmanuel Akinseloyin (Kampusflowztv), Afia Akpan,

Opeyemi Ogunbiyi, Gabriel Onyekwelue, Donald Awalite, Ifeoluwa Ifekoya and Chikwendu Onyeoziri of blessed memory.

Special thanks to Reverend Yomi Kasali for years of stoic mentorship.

And special thanks to Pedro Omontuemhen for his large heart and his ebullient spirit.

Special shout out to Babatunde Tofunmi for all the moments of literary and tech disquisitions; I say cheers to the plethora of great things to come.

And to the memory of a beloved shepherd, Pastor Ajayi; I remember most of the songs you sang of deep spiritual essence and the others, I just extrapolate the lyrics. Your memory is blessed.

Special thanks to Tolu' A. Akinyemi, the Lion of Newcastle; for all the love, belief, support, magnanimity and time spent to run through the manuscript. You have a place in the solemn, albeit, boisterous temple of my heart. I really appreciate you.

Special thanks to all the literary and digital platforms that have lent good hands to this craft: Tuesday poems, Dami Ajayi; Redlletterconcept.com; Toluakinyemi.com; Griots and Bards, Rezthapoet; Wordup411, Olulu; Freedom hall, Tope Saiq; Lagos Book and Art Festival, Jahman Anikulapo; Wordaholics, Komolafe Komsons, Savannah Poets, Dipo; and Chisom, Loudthotz, Lion and Lilac, and Lagos Poetrython.

PREFACE

I have always marvelled at how words lubricate the human spirit with joy and the fortitude to ply the hysteric alley of life with ever-bubbling gusto. I have also come to understand the burden of those who employ effectual words to disarm or enamour people. Men of old summoned words to their rescue in every duel of survival where the deft use of words is the only accessory to conquest.

To me, words are sacred, potent, and energetic—the whole crux of manifestations of events in this sphere consists of the forcible nature of words, hence, I do not take for granted or discard in hurry, words that are fitly spoken.

Although I will always fling to the gouge of disgust, with oomph alacrity, words that sap bones of nutritious marrow. I will gladly sit at the bilge in any assembly where words are effulgently woven to capture the essence of everyday life, and the meaning of this unavoidable cross called breath, just to enjoy the cutting-edge adventure in the lush forest of words.

Sometimes, words give me the gripping sensations of pareidolia, and till this moment, I am daily stung by the magical fangs of words and stupefied by their eclectic hold on man…

Words came to me in my early years; hence, the poem, *Poet tree,* in this collection and would literally morph into something poignant. I could touch, romanticize, and imagine all scenarios imbued in both perspicuous and oblique conversations shrouded in words.

I have also tried to slake my yearning for precise words to describe literal impressions by constipating on a handful of novels and every available literary piece in my way and yet leap like a child at Disneyland when I hear the news of any enthralling new literary arrival in town that will wet my curiosity with new delight.

I remember that, at one time, I interrogated everything on my path in the light of words and viscerally queried the furnace of intentions that set them ablaze for a reckoning. And I still do.

I have always looked forward to the day this accosting vapour of words would be condensed and bottled up in a papery jar. I am so happy we are here.

This collection of poems attempts to touch every aspect of human experience. It brings to fore the burdens, joy, laughter, hope and expectations of everyday people and also jabs at the misconduct of the rule against the ruled. I also did experimentation on form and syntax and just wrote from observations to give readers a swell time purring through the works. I drew inspiration from all humans on the Maslow's pyramid.

Well, this is my maiden collection, and I hope you find something amazing and fitting for your interest in this self-effacing and candid collection.

POEMS

I have learned how to live

I drown my silk hair in the soothing strokes of rainfall,
lashes curled by the talons of the garrulous wind.
I trapped rainwater in crooked potsherds for Grandma so we
      could make our favourite swallow and wash the dross
      of anxiety off the filaments of my skin.

I watch the sun slump into a boundless void, with mouth
      agape.
I unburden my soul, confessions of affection unrequited.
Piled-up loans against hunger trailing the serrated lines in my
      hopeful palms.
I eschewed the ragged snares of regret with the plea of grateful
      dispositions,
floated in the wind of outrageous dreams and contracted
      succour from waiting—
      waiting for an economic angel,
      waiting for the cornrow of gladness to sprout,
      waiting for the rainbow while drifting in the garrulous
      storm.

I gauge the fairness of time with my fingers dipped in
the lively billows of crooked ashes and chew memories
that dangle by the blades of anxious longing.
My mind abhors songs of sorrow or any tide of emotions
stuck in the pond of disgust.
Day by day, beyond bytes, likes
and retweets, I have learned how to live.

Curly smoke

In the curly smoke of herbal intelligence/at the backdrop of stubborn flies frolicking the fractured/shades of a twinkling lantern behind the silhouette of Africa/sifting through parchments and bodies/interrogating science and incantations/scouting leaves and names for potions in the dark throes of a pandemic/grinding roots, shrubs and specks of dust to soluble/juxtaposing the spatial plains of herbal formula/lisping frail expletives hyphenated by grievous tut-tutting atop the mortuaries of acquaintances/inflamed by the swoosh of blooming, gouging apothecaries/At sunrise, underneath the bamboo bed of sweat and study/she cradled the seven kettles of vaccines for the healing of all nations/Freighted to the ends of the Earth by the waltzing hashtags across new media/about the efficacy of the curly smoke of African herbal intelligence/and verified by the memes of convalescing witnesses

Requiem in paradise

We held a requiem in paradise,
trailing kites of fond memories like grounded drifters.
Our indifference to medical advice had begun to give way
        under the torrential onslaught of this monstrous
        pandemic.
We clung to the root of hope, tethered to the anguish of
broken silver cords
and lay siege on the closing clouds of faith to bring a token of
        good for this depressing harvest of bones.
We held a requiem in paradise,
praying for this tumultuous darkness to leave the spotlight.

Convalescence

At the break of day, my ego, with bruises from the hurt of unrequited affection, stood at the porch of your heart, draped in the sparkles of the beads of light that sat on your aquiline nose, calling at the benevolence of your acceptance into the fortress of your embrace.

We open

When dispersed seeds amongst stones and thorns
crave the tingling skin of light to fulfil their cause,
they scratch a way out, upturning all encumbrances with their
        brittle sprouts.
They spread themselves in the waft of bliss for a feast on the
        scrumptious wheat of sunlight.

When flowery plants in pursuit of expression crack the womb
of the soil to bloom,
the soil opens; it opens to interrogate the plants' bravery;
it grovels at their pulchritude.

The nimble Venus Flytrap trapped by sordid ants opens to
        crush the intruders in its halo.

And when the psychotic knees of obnoxious racists
doodle blatant epilogues of black lives growing daisies at the
        glare of a reprobate world, we open.

We open to unearth the umbilical cord of black lives across
        geographies.
We open to aerate the stinking catacombs of wrath wrung by
        the festering sores of racial injustice,

we open to plait the cold cord of nostalgia into knotted nooses
        of decimation for
chattels, neo-colonialism, drudgery and systemic racism,
we open to write the narratives of our lives, values, valour,
        ancestry, triggers and time.

Kindness

I snatched you from your ominous blanket of dreary dreams
and removed the veil of horror from the floundering
iris of this drifting man in the mirror.
I drew the disparaging wool of dystopia out of your aching
          ears and
let the earth refuse your crustacean scurry to the fortress of
          blandness.
I watch your name become a distillery of tongues
wagging moisturized chants to list your
right to a lease of a borderless life.

A life stuffed with goodness,
I am the kind waterfall of arms
bringing utensils of the living to the forlorn home of travailing
          hearts.

Abiku

You are the itchy hair of velvet bean,
the estuary of stranded skeletons.
You are a lacustrine plain bereft of the sediments of mirth.
You drown mouths in tears,
grease faces with the unctuous stream of drivel.
You toggle between the tombs of hubris and weary wombs,
you deflate gravid bellies with needles of woe,
decorating your mothers' lean cheeks with the mascara of
        wretchedness.

You are the dance of anxious waves on meaningless
        peregrination,
every bloody clutter of marks on your earmarked remains is
        our wistful ebb of silence.

Moribund restaurant

In this glittering and moribund restaurant called *Naija*,
      hunger dies of lack!
Yesterday's sour meals of sordid stories are still on today's
      menu,
the maggot-ridden appetizers of money-laundering cuisine are
      strung on the white linen thoughts of national
      prosperity.
Political pests continually finger and break into the lump of
      our national pudding with their greed-infected
      fingers.
Economic rodents stool and run our resources aground.
These chefs are the lords of mischief,
stirring the concoctions of vast affluence with the blood
and other grievous condiments of the downtrodden.
These morsels of tongue-in-cheek campaigns,
extolling nepotism, marginalisation, apathy,
inciting tribal delicacies may yet be our last supper.

Shark tale

17th of January, 2012 at 1:44pm

The volume swallows my throw
as a crowd overwhelms a miniature.
Several rotten heads and faded bones parade
themselves for a wanderer's pictures.
Hello, Mr Shark,
you ruled this coast and ate men into ghosts.
Their blood, you sprinkled as toast.
Several ships you tumbled and the carcass, you towed.
I've got a coin,
hooked to my loins,
this ocean I seek to purloin.
The coins, my mascot to excavate treasures of worth
but the ocean winks sinisterly,
bidding me come.
I press on her bidding,
forewarned by tales of drowned sailors
yet the resources on this coast I want to capture.
I know life is an ocean,

sharks, obnoxious circumstances.
Still, I will plunge into this ocean.
When I look, my strength skips,
but I will watch as the shark's jaws clutch.
Blood may sprinkle from my vein so much,
but the golden fleece is worth a fight as such.
These glistening treasures of light and sweet smiles,
I will fight to have them fall in line.
Hope last dies, though toss tough like contoured dice.
Hope grants life twice.
Within the clavicle of a dauntless spirit, hope cries loud.

First kiss

29th of May, 2010 at 3:01am

My whole being quaked
My smiles, garrisoned by dimples, grew wide
Her desired stains my lips cannot hide
On my feet, I glide sheepishly
I blush, my mouth never to brush in a rush
But nurse in reminiscence of her lips' touch
This memory from my soul will never be flushed
Her oval lips closing on my waiting lips
Felt like Chinese chips
Our souls were set ablaze and ignited in delight
My smitten soul had a red-letter thread on Twitter
The drama, my loveliest screensaver
She stirred my spirit to soar and my wobbling strides to roar
My muscles rippled like the chattering of a million people
My heartbeat skipped as my faith leapt
For this truth
As a memoir of our hook
In an ambience of bliss
Gently in bits
I had my first kiss.

Love's soothing web

14ᵗʰ of February, 2013

Her translucent eyes whisper into my ears
tales of nimble affection,
weaving paradise of happiness in my heart.

I see your eyes twinkling brighter than sunlight's rays.
I wonder why my soul never ceased into them to pry.
You are one of a kind, and in your heart, I find tenderness.
In your eyes hangs the constellation of stars
dispelling the terror of damp and lonesome nights.

Let our heart in the truth of what we share find affectionate
        symmetry.
Take me to the ecstatic sphere where desirous
heaves and moans condense into the raucous
tides of a consummated symphony.
I will love you until the night no longer fills up the forest;
let your embrace be my coolest stay.

Laughter

Let the curves of disgust part as the Red Sea
Let the teeth as bright as the colour of the silvery moon be
Let the mountains of your worries crumble like the walls of
Jericho
Wear joy as an ornament on the navel of your soul
Let laughter cascade down your spine like
The sparkling cackles of Niagara Falls
Let it escape your lips as a free bird
Let it moisturize your heart and chisel your
Cheeks with the bubbles of waterspouts
There is a ritzy sheriff in town with some smiley canisters
Commit a laugh and be handcuffed and let behind the bars of
inescapable joy!

White Mark has got a tribal mark

Ribs crack,
hands dip into laughter's mockery sack
as we recall White Mark and his tribal marks.
With his head, stern and straight like a soldier in a parade,
the wild lines infect his smile with a slippery calm,
the marks crack his lofty climb.
I condensed flat into seizures of serial pranks.
White Mark has tribal marks!
An awful stigma, like the blatant sadness on the blurred face of
        a tethered ram.
Deeper and spiral went the mark in clutter.
Grotesque cheeks. Racist quibbles. Supremacist banter.
His eyes stroll with the pace of a shoddy shoe,
leaking the insecurities of pigmentation.
His imperial blush steeply washes,
his fat, complex splashes in colonial verses.
When a White man wears tribal marks,
his ego festers the rottenness in the silk marrow of humanity,
enabling the vile dynasty of human chattel,
stirring the rage of racial animosity.

Naked soul

I bare my heart to you; before you I am naked.
I walk with abandon on the strings of your sugar-coated
        promises,
hope that what you seek isn't emotional asylum in the name of
        love?

Tell the White man

Quarrying black blood from gaunt skulls in sweat-littered
          mines, mining pain from the hollows of dead hearts
as ships meander Africa's artefacts and diamonds past the
          Nile.
Tell the White man that the Black man will make your dreams
          work.

Incinerate revolutionary tongues and pluck the
brittle and flowery memories of our Sankaras and Gaddafis.
Tell the White man that the Black man will make your dreams
          work.

Mud-sling the African gods to enthrone Zeus,
Hermis, Arthemes and the White lot.
Tell the White man that the Black man will make your dreams
          work.

Fling Black migrants who grope for greener pastures
across the seas into the gallows of misery,
bury them in the cesspit of slavery.
Tell the White man that the Black man will make your dreams
          work.

Make a spectacle of the cruel waves of
the Mediterranean and snuff the life out of prodigal dreamers.
Tell the White man that the Black man will make your dreams
          work.

Loan them lame pills for the imperialists,

induce economic scourge to make their stupefied minds the
dumping ground for your medical experiments.
Tell the White man that the Black man will make your dreams
work.

Dance to the incoherent rhythm of their development
while you mock the obsolescence of their leadership and
deadbeat economic percussions.
Tell the White man that the Black man will make your dreams
work.

Trade your prescient technology to nip the sovereignty of
Black nations.
But tell the White man that the Black man will make your
dreams work.

Noose and die

His slippery words swept her feet like banana peels;
she fell and slipped into a nine-month conundrum.
Her name sprung up everywhere like a repulsive dictum.

She was berated by every tongue
and was asked why she sat her baseline on his turgid member
        in a hurry.
"Why fall for his well-spun promises of a nuptial affair?"
 Her sanity was wrecked in the tempest of their malicious din.

She buried her troubled head in flames of weeds
to suppress her fears.
She gulps cups of lemonade to exorcise the demons in her
        mind.

But the demons grew muscles and pounced on her insecurities
        more and more.
She became sick and pale like worn-out fabric.
She began to avoid the tongue-wagging gatherings of
        hypocrites.

The vicious voices mounted a rostrum of
slut-shaming on her mistake and filled her thoughts with
        regrets, saying:

Tie and die
and your worries will be no more.
Tie and die
and your pains will cease like water from a closed tap.
Tie and die

and the embroidery of your misery will never glow.
     Tie and die
and your shame will be gone.

She grabbed some yellow pills
     to appeal her guilt.

I didn't rest in peace, her last note read.
This place hurts so much. I need a rest.

How to hate Cupid

Drown your heart in the wretched lime of unwholesome
   bickering
Do not make convalescent lemonade of your scars
Weigh every prospect with the rear mirror of your misery
Distil your disappointment in the caustic heaves of
   lonesomeness
Contract hyperkalemia from the whimsical toast to the relics
   of your obsession
Pelt self-loathing tantrums on the scarecrow of your
   insecurities
Linger by the sepulchre of your lover's dead butterflies
Aerate the stinking essays of lust over love on the stool of
   regrets
Marinate your soul with the pus of despair
Break the pans in your living room, slam the creaking door
   and hit your leg against The innocent bouquet of grey
   flowers for romantic flashbacks
Envy lovebirds with blooming affections
Wait to be badly slit by the oval shards of love
Square your grief
Laugh at yourself
Mock your shame
Gnaw at your friends
Decry your gut to cry
Wail
Don't breathe
Drip mucus while you faint
Wake up
Sneeze
Hoodwink your peace

Be emotionally vain
Nurse not the twirling sutures of your despondence
Speak to the wall, wood and mirror about your shock, guilt
      and abuse
Do not lick the dew that drips the good tidings of a resurgence
Refuse to reset the settee and portraitures of a new dawn in the
      room of your soul
Frown at the dark rays of your setting gloom
Demonize the petrichor of emotional rebirth
Meander the dark alleys of dementia
Box your ailing memory in the cold room of amnesia
Enjoy blackouts

Falling child

Torn clothes
Seemingly nice mistress
Panties-pulling master
Cheeks as mortar for pounding abuse
Head for iron-belt, canes, and a myriad of flying objects
Aladdin's lamp of wishes
Disparaged pilgrim of the quotidian nightmarish dusk
Hollow of endless fears
Whitlow-ridden fingers
Neck pressed by burdens
Fantasy of misery
Scarred body from needless beatings
Burgled ivory of chastity
Stitched smiles
Night-crawler of chores
Day-walker of garbage
Deadbeat epicurean
Daydreamer of ease
Grand-mistress of tribulations
Amazon of insomniacs
A falling child

For Modupe Cole and all the schools for special kids

(Autism and co)

We pray to God for blessings,
But he gave us more than our yearnings—

Lips caressing words like fingers on rosaries.
These beautiful ones are wrapped with thorns, but they bloom
   as roses.

Some are restless as leaves on troubled water,
For the strength of many gods is caged in them.

They are the ellipsis of a running rainbow,
The intersection of desire and question marks.

We beg to unravel the layers of their humanity as
One who gently stacks grains of heaves upon heaps of sigh.

And for every time we beg for a reconstruction of their
   dispositions in the name of a miracle,
We know that these special ones are the seedlings of miracles.

We pray to God for blessings,
He gave us more than our yearnings.

Merchant of iniquity

Grace on a reprobate mind
The rustler of the dross-clotted armour of faux spirituality
Auctioneer of the shroud of vicissitudes
Unapologetic trojan of paraplegic productivity
Tastebud of a barren womb
The valve of haunted thoughts
Restless lids of a schemer
Gracious lord of abuse
Integral of fitly filthy elocution
Calculus of teething ventricles of supplication
Vanguard of the tenets of servitude and impotent religious
      leaning
A watchman of coin-tossing gamblers beneath a castrated
      cross
Cloud of hyperreal expectations
A subtle exponent of the fiefdom of righteousness
Crusader of apocalyptic wrath
A conductor of the grovelling orchestra of wantonness
Soiled palms
Randy iris
Jackpot of tantrums
Jetsam of peace
Don of liminal lingering
Bane of celestial benevolence
Bishop of white sepulchres
Merchant of iniquity

She is not yours

24th of October, 2018

Ten o'clock at night,
Her *uncle* comes online.
She peels away from you,
Her voice on the phone is tepid and low.

Her energy for the night is not yours,
She sideswipes your chivalry with a smirk.

She is not yours.
You can only wish.
The sordid night blurs her memories of you,
The wick of her soul is averse to the effervescent fire of your
          desire
And like the green grass on the other side, she never was
          yours.

Dust arise

Love is God asking dust to rise.
Love is a storm bowing before a solemn touch.
Love is the knob of an empty home
forsaken by hearts who once quenched
their thirst from its refreshing fountain.

Love is the lighthouse for lingering hearts.
Love is a porter, lifting burdens that break its arms and will to
          satisfy longings.
Love is a good Samaritan, exchanging kindness for nothing.
Love is a spiritual epiphany,
the water brook of wholesomeness for contrite souls.

If I had wings like a dove

If I had wings like a dove,
I would perch on the roof of your conscience and
remind you not to sell your vote.
Else, the muttering lips of the next generation would
submit that servitude was a fine ornament on
the crooked neck of your soul.

If I had wings like a dove,
I would bring the moon and stars to the corridors of
your soul to remind you not to permit the
darkness of your need to cast blindness on the eye of your
        thumb.

If I had wings like a dove,
I would perch by the window of your heart and
ask you to avoid the disastrous economic meteorologists,
political physicians of no value and the sixteen
packs of money-voracious wolves beneath a leaking
umbrella in the rainstorm of greed and regret.

If I had wings like a dove,
I would pinch you not to transpose the
election day to your funeral date.
It isn't a good day for you to die.
Just needless political callisthenics of foolishness.

If I had wings like a dove.
I would make a nest of your head and
request that you exercise empathy while you
vote for our collective destiny and rake a revolution.

Old

When I become old,
I will leap whenever the night croaks,
Sight the languid, laughing cheekbones of stillbirths,
Pluck my peeving eyes from prancing hips,
Lisp the paeon of the rescinding darkness of desire on my lips.

When I become old,
I will frown at hazy, lazy, crazy morns,
Yell at the tick-tock wall of gasping time,
Mock my wheezing breath
And relish each interring day.

When I become old,
I will name the stars with the memories of fallen friends,
Smell with nostalgia the wreaths for the decoration of my
        skeleton,
Ignore the tantrums of crickets, houseflies and age-long
        domestic foes,
Yawn anytime the truth is cheaply sold.

When I become old,
I will crave less for superfluous kindness,
Wink a smile at serpentine acquaintances,
Despise the reckless leeches of inheritances,
Brush the bush hair of posterity.
When I become old,
I will make more storms of teacups,
Make wishy-washy wishes to all would-be wailers,
Wait till this breath will cease with a kiss from eternity
And hope that in yonder, the heavenly bosom of the celestials
        will be cleft for me.

Shadows of the evening

I

I crave a life not less or even,

to celebrate life with a feast of bread not so leavened.

I ate ambitious bread of little leaven,

drank wine and slept with shoes opposite the shadows of
eleven kettles.

I skated the clouds of snowy desires,

tore gold out of wild animals in the forest of pursuits,

surfed on a green plateau, and ruled the creeks of dreams.

II

In the umbra of days, I grew in the thistles of hard work;

I know the pain of eating hot yams without a fork.

I have seen wrinkles in days; same as the limp lines like trunks
on this face,

they stood with gloom and grace.

I had grown in days; in its hysteria stream, I ate and bathe.

III

In the penumbra of thoughts,

I shivered in cold, fondled the memories of days when on me
it had no hold.

When in its chilling grip, my strength excelled in flips but now
it has my spines.

I beared its grip with fear and wine.

IV

In the penumbra of sight,
I had seen mountains morph into plain grounds
and dry rivers puff into the ocean.
Tempestuous hays incurred peace and the skies lent warmth to
        the rainbow of indomitable effort.
The rains spat resurrection on crooked soil
and days yet yawn; the firmament remains as firm as that of
        when I was born.

V

In the shadows of the evening, lurk
the memories of frightful friends and faithful foes, stolen bread
        and stillborn hopes.
When the shadows of the hasty evening overshadow the
        corridors of existence,
desires adore frailty, and fear punks the heart of the caravans
        of pursuit.
Desires linger past the cave of emptiness, fingering through
        the cardinals of
un-scored goals, cherished misses, wholesome
        sores, comforting pain and favoured regrets.

In the dark claws of the shadows of the evening, life oozes,
        bereaved of days.

Lagos is killing me

Her pinches I whistle in loud whispers
Of men in economic diapers
Manhood an allegory of blunt clippers
This Lagos explodes in my head like a million firecrackers
Lagos is killing me!
I comb grave nooks in the hustle
Getting a bus, a fistful bustle
Yet no seat to settle
My lean purse I vigorously cuddle
Lest I tell the tale of my vagrant money
Not a soul blinks with pity
Only a loud *mtchewww*
Lagos is killing me!
Curses slap your face
For legs tripped over in disdain
For the day's sterile race
In the nascence of the day
Lagos wears rainbow
Flies black when the curve of your economy is bent into a bow
Lagos has got no weather
Lagos is a rambunctious hooker
She dates all souls
Even aliens
Lagos is bending me
The neck of my polo she slacks
Lack dulled my notion of great meals
A sure handful of Garri is better than dreams of tasty snacks
All flesh is mortal
The soul of Lagos is immortal
Defining your grandest style beneath your epitaph

Humans pay rent in plank duplexes sited on heaps
With germs, reptiles and termites, rooms are fully occupied
Existence of maintenance bills
Keep you on self-medicated pills
Landlord stacks you with a quit notice
You roll out like a rotten yam on the bin
Lagos is a friendly bully
Friendly to new notes of crisp naira
A bully to sagging pockets of rusty kobo
Lagos is a gambler
She taught me how to play lotto
To play and win, I sold my motor
I lost, she mailed me to her ghetto

Lagos is killing me
I am a frustrated Lagosian
I am an untrained physician
Trained in the school of upset-brain
I will inject your health strains
Just to get my pay
Don't care if you are 'okay'
Lagos is killing me
I am a grumbler on the injured street in the cheerful city of
          Lagos
I pay for the blackouts
My folks have gone to weed-out
Some, out of sheer helplessness, passed out of reality to
          illegality
Embracing the purity of insanity
Lagos killed them
I know the spirit of Lagos
It's called 'Hustle'
I trek to save cost

In heaviness, tears out of my face burst
I took advice from bubbling bottles
I sleep with my eyes careful
Insomnia, my pride in Lagos
In my head, she sizzles like minced meats
Her classy fares I drag in a mire to meet
In the heat of my bustle, I pause and kneel
I made confessions about this Lagos that steals my sanity
Lagos is killing me!

Cowries

Radiant cowries of the esteemed African pride,
what wonders, your prudence as a virtuous bride.
For centuries, you were a potent economic catalyst,
measuring the value of wares on behalf of our kind ancestors.
Your skilled painting in crystal milk by nature gives you a cosy
       look—
a symbol of peace, respect and sincerity immersed in
       moderation.
Mindful of the mood, capacity and class of hagglers,
distant from greed, extortion or apparitions of economic vice.
Your weighty size amplifies your image and stand
amongst numerous currencies of diverse nations,
your enchanting serrated buttons enrapture the world
in speechless glee at your sassy outfit.
Your blessed gift of composite functions and
pristine socioeconomic design by nature
makes you a wonder to several merchants.
You give lustre to the tunics of hunters and
exquisite antiquity to modern-day fashion.
Kids are kept at sea at your glitz,
Elders pay homage to your durability,
the world salutes your unique frame
held in the palms of shrewd descents, peasants and aristocrats,
you remain dauntlessly relevant to the specifics of race and
       voices,
you are indeed an ancient seed of awesome merchandise and
       ritzy fashion.

Earth days

I didn't have much; I stood behind a church,
plead for a few crumbs to munch, but my moth-eaten clothes
          they mocked.
My frailty and stinking shorts, they scorned; I plead, even in
          pains.
I cried and coughed when my voice grew faint, yet not a soul
          came to my aid.
Even when I lay in the sun with no shade,
they walked through with a kind-less gaze; not of will that I am
          wealth-weak;
the mystery of lack transcends my being.
I attended funerals, garrisoned by stone-cold generals.
I ate meals, amidst dogs and pigs, to say of a truth;
my meals were never worthy of meats, the waiters thought too
          less of me,
with less kind words, they reminded me of me: the lesser me,
          sorry me.
My tables were never high.
Only in distress, I go high.
I leave gatherings with no thanks; they abhor my stay like I
          lead an army of sick fangs.
I fell sick of existence, to all woes and her sisters.
I fell sick of the kind-less church
Hypocrites! Who loves not their brothers, let alone
          neighbours?
I fell sick of life, the false balances of its favour,
not often giving wheat to wisdom.
I fell sick of carrying this soul with appalling sores.
Vexed in the mire of shame and failure that
I had crawled in, I besought the celestials for mercy,

I embraced the cold hands of the damp night for refuge,
and snoring in its torrential palms,
I had a life-less sleep.
I couldn't have asked for more, the stench of
my swollen carcass announced my death.
Buried in the stomach of eagles, dogs and insects,
I had my piecemeal rest.
This soul was given a befitting funeral, absent of
religious generals, nor pretentious faithful.
No prayers were said to end my earth days,
except the blessings on my carcass they ate.
Loud spits and hisses bathe my remains.
The empathy of soiled-garment saints, they cared not if I lived.
There are more like me behind your doors, in misery in their
         earth days.
In your hands their hopes lie, will you bless their day?

Sweet mother

Like a lump in her womb was my seed in her tube,
washing her skin into the mottled pigment of a St Louis cube,
invoking amidst her being a strange feud,
as the odd presence of a teetotaller in a pub.
Her feet clogged with the weight of the beach,
sands swinging her waist in unfair balance,
her mouth wanes as murky streams in holes,
cut-out in cones, insipid like a meal of sour bones.
Her words in slurry mime, sticky as reptilian slime.
My birth an awaited grace, shutting her face in the theatre of
          bizarre fate.
Clock ticks slowly, moments drag excessively,
the pangs of death shrill loudly.
Darkness crests her shoulders, a weakness she shuddered,
her eyes flapping like papery shutters,
a form within troubles for the world to see,
in a minute, the ethereal world she sojourned,
the energy of bliss in tears to summon.
In her head were sparks of devastating lightning,
submerging her world in ferocious imageries.
As I tore through her tissues into the entreating hands in
          queue,

yet her silver cord launched forth my umbilical cord
as the letting of rope to a kite to soar.
Her life against death's stake, to hold my fragile frame.
All just stood in awry gaze as, in the world, I took my place.
Of her pains to have me stay, she never complained,
but a smile and kiss for all the agony in wait.
So, this convener of my frame is the most famous of all being
            of fame,
for my soul on the sands of time,
she compelled to stay.

Naija Wahala

Your fat economy was the ecstasy of colonialism,
neocolonialism corrupts your plains as the
continuous rape on a hypnotized damsel.
Your seeds are sown as weeds in foreign soils,
their flowers plucked with unkind might,
the wheat of their sweat they seldom receive to bless,
adorned in servile manacles, crumbs are a miracle.
You wreathed in pains of appalling unity,
the sham of peace in unity, more war in cultural diversity.
Ethnocentrism in a perpetual struggle for
the coronation to the oval office of affluence.
Deceit scarify the hospice of tribal warmth,
plunged into the typhoon of distraught amalgamation,
masked in militancy, help is sought from its tortuous grip.
O Nigeria, your eyes sink behind their sockets,
they sag of sorrow, caught from rival turbulence of your
            frenzied heirs.
You sail in the illusion of progress without
covering distances as the still tapping of a crushed cricket
            without legs.
Babies in power, the *wahala* of Nigeria.
Scums in palaces, the palaver of Africa.
Your green goes grey in the blood-letting hands of
Ill-will folks who warm your globe with infectious growth,

riddled with malaria, taking showers in the raucous rain of
       cholera,
the inmates in the cell of noisome wants hoard the healing
       naira.
They fan their own yam on fire with the nation's palm.
They lick all the oil with crème men on our soil.
From this mental fever of greed growing fonder,
you will someday be delivered.
To this offensive scourge, we will find a cure.
I stand to see you through until our purpose is true,
and our anthem of truth.
Wait.
Just wait.
The revolutionary doctor comes in the
whirlwind of scattered scatteredness and trumps
the revenge of men in tatters, pelting livid
curses at those who sell their ancestral lands,
and the destructive rambles of children in torn pants,
wailing, *why?*
Revolution has envisioned our land; soon,
it will infiltrate with a merciless entourage,
to give us a new age, a new page in the history of time.
Yes, a cure to the *wahala* of Nigeria.

"Wahala" is synonymous with "palaver."

Poet tree

I sat on the wit of a poet tree
I read lines in pages of poetic letters in a light- and power-
        acquisition spree
On several burning notes, we agree
Poetry like a pear tree, we pick rhymes for free
Our clothed nakedness, we lucidly see
The nakedness of nothingness
The nothingness of existence
Our persistence in existence
Hovering across the essence of existence and the sense in
        existence
I chew one-tenth of sane tenses that interpret the essence of
        joy-bereft sentences
I bit the fruit of ethereal depth on the poet tree, in chapters
        and verses
I marked oxymoron on my speech tree
Antithesis I chew for a gift

My pulse less understood by morons, the voice of sarcasm
        became clarion

The axe of pain is oxy
The hook of forgiveness is a moron
I sat on the trunk of pun
It lulls my bum-bum with fun
I swung next to a paradox
Like a good father does, bestowing kindness that opens doors
On the poet tree, I and wisdom had tea, knowledge obliged me
Understanding took me to fish
I sketched the mural of this three on a baobab tree
I sang the ode of this three on a poet tree
On a poet tree, my life from the regrets of yesterday became
        free
On the poet tree, swirls the personification of poetry

Orita meta

Table of dark providence
The crux of esoteric callisthenics
An intersection of mortal intents and celestial acquiescence
Hydra-headed pathway of hyperventilated supplication
Intermesh of yearnings and surreal providence
Valley of hungry beings feeding robust demons
A collision of junctions to lend potency to the matrix of
       human longings
The orbit of the crooked potsherds of fortune
The plain of darkness, despising the numeracy of light
The stratosphere of succour to wayward burdens and
       perennial plights
The assemblage of clay pots, firestorms, offertory, palm oils,
       wickedness and repercussions.
Orita meta!

Uneasy calm

Slumbering dreams
Hope deferred
Brave resolves
Cold embrace
Elixir of faith
Star-bereft skies
Moonless nights
Friendly injuries
Fiendish warmth
Gorgeous penury
Effortless fortune
Withering flowers
Blooming weeds
Such is LIFE.

Fearless

We are the never dis-spirited conqueror
Our spirits rise from slumber before the ebbs of the morning
            tides
High spirit begets a sound body while sheepish minds will
            remain the long-awaited guests of nobody
We hold our grind at the arduous base of the threshing floor
We caress hope in the darkest moment of looming defeats
In rags, yet we dream of robes of many colours
We chew happiness out of crumbs
Have our bath in our sweat
Fill our thirst from anorexic fountains
Sleep in the comfort of thunderstorms in the wilderness of
            pursuit
Feed on creepy insects but our will was trojan
Drowned in the rivers of loneliness
Smote by wary arrows of despair
Entertained by the horrific notes of the dust-crusted rhythm of
            the faceless night
Contended with the depressing angels of affliction
But the bruises of our expectations are healed from the herbs
            of grit

53

Fondled by the frostbite of the Harmattan
Discouraged at no point in time
Beaten by fate, yet risen in faith
Heaven resides in us
But hell, in those who dream but will not pursue
Dreams pamper the eyelids of the snoring soul
Nightmares set them awake to work
Dreams visit as friends
Nightmares as hard-faced strangers
In trials, muscles we grow
In triumph, we trim the scars from stumbling blocks
We set purpose towards a life as seductive as paradise
But sleep in odoriferous lakes of venomous reptile and planet
          of hideous monsters
Our face is fixed on conquest as the stars
Life is a dream
An unfaithful stream
Bids all to come to her bounteous inn
But no one leaves without kicking the bucket.

She has a next

Love skipped this memory like a forgotten league
Lust accosted me with its hypnotic armoury of lucre
I hit my injection needle on six-times-three ladies
All came out for a play in our bash of carnal revelry
Love now parades my soul with drums of whistling tragedy
The tragedy of a broken heart
This soul is afraid of getting a fraction for a whole
A fraction of beans for a whole bean sack
I gave my best for the least of her affection
I was crucified on her tree of inordinate selection
She asked for gold
Told her my dreams will yield treasures fearsomely bold
My hays she scorned
Asked if I could hawk corn
She ripped my heart and fed the ventricles to lust
My heart, in grief, had its nest—
The pain of knowing she has a next
My worries unearthed from the deepest layers of
          lonesomeness
I withdrew the memories of fun in my head
I lowered the graffiti of her lips, hips, beads and fun skits
In the template of my heart, I lit the canvas of her beauty to
          ashes
Blew wild and tormented kisses to her being
I shivered as I kissed score bottles to her memory in demise
Her frame yet has its lustrous grip on my brain
I wheeled her memory into the wilderness of amnesia
Mnemonics of love in my heart for tales I keep
In this being, love skipped the heart for a sabbatical
Leave and never to return until the master wills

With kings in Colorado

I scarcely wear designers
I never lost the hope of making cash to flash
I have no shoes with the sole of Prada
It does not lessen my swagger
Just at the party gates, gives me a small palaver
And for my lean pocket
Eyes bulge in the sunken socket
No cash to fondle the blooms in dangling brackets
Fortune bestows me kindness not as such
I loathe this broke life so much
A feet gladiator, I kill stress
I become a compulsive narrator of one-eyed tales
Sharp pains massage my feet
As I roam the street in a mess
I spend words during the feast
I dance with concern about the top I borrowed
I pocket my locket of dreams with superfluous laughter and
          tripping folly
In awkward shoes, I stretch in the steps of a pony
I sip for long hours, my shot of whiskey from a Samaritan
I shiver when classic Stella winks at me
In my delirium, I wear a Tuxedo
I eat with kings in Colorado
In my broke days
I had no rights but blames
I often bury my head in shame
But the ember of hope in me still had its flames
I smile, though it's a painful makeover
I crouch by the desert of joy as I watch the sandstorm
Of hope fling my fears into the oasis of serendipity

Colour-riot days

3ʳᵈ of August, 2012

On sweet blue days,
I fell in love with fair-colour maids with lustrous lashes of
      cartoon mermaids.
On yellow days, I wore black sun shades, Ray-Ban made
On dark days, loneliness cuddling hysteria broke into
chaotic songs of liberty and lends chariot to the voices in my
      head.

On black days,
like fog is everything man-made:
German cars. Egyptian paintings. Chinese pomade and the
      manifesto of Nigerian politicians.

Mostly on light Thursdays,
I throw back the awkward memories of barbarian days.

On broke days,
men with purses in red found a duty to pray.
On rainbow days,
with salsa dance, pretty lasses we dazed,
as we split our pants and swoon to the bipedal moon-walk of
      Michael Jackson's *Thriller.*

On black days,
life is an unfair trade, favours all with six-feet grade.

On colour-riot days,
I enjoy rants by Jamaican brides wearing scattered Norwegian
      braids
and African ladies, flipping Peruvian wigs as they loaf behind
      the carousel of loathsome neo-colonial trends.

Ibirikembiri, Live and Let Us Live

i
Fake drug peddlers
The castles of your wealth
Is in the multiplicity of our death
Our failing health
The loudness of your cheers
Our peeling flesh
Keeps your supplies fresh
May your joy be infested with strange boils!

ii
Jaundiced politicians
You chant strange manifestoes
Would they keep mosquitoes off our homes?
You promise us tomorrow
Our trust you borrow
Yet our reward is never less than sorrow
Evident in your loots
That could have bettered our luth
Build more luths
Repair our routes
Revamp our schools
As you have become a burden
May the flower of your economic fever start budding.

iii
Men in glass houses
You roast elephants
Yet you pick our ants
You sleep in refined rooms
The fumes of your plants heat our dreams
And litter our sleep with filth
May your forehead be kissed with cholera in bits!

iv
Vagabonds in power
You detain the poor
At the feet of corporate criminals, you fall
You ask a dying man why he stole
Asked you if he had hope?
May the ropes in gallows become attractive to your soul.

v
Men of integrity
For a change, you sweat
Knives of criticism you embraced into your chest
Your headaches with loads of cares
Till your heart explodes into shreds of tears
Posterity will cover your humanity
As your statue of liberty lives on in our memory
And the torch of your struggle translates into the compass of
          our destiny.

Love Nwa Tin Tin

Her translucent eyes whisper to my ears
tales of nimble affection.
Weaving an aesthetic paradise of happiness in my heart
like the triangular draft of a spider.

I see your eyes,
the flustering splendour is brighter than the crisp sparkles of
       stars.
I wonder why my soul never ceased into them to pry.

You are one of a kind,
in your heart, the mine of tenderness I find.

With adventure, your world I will roam
till your pulse flips and pauses in Rome.

Your kiss I linger for lease,
a thousand years at least.

In your eyes are hidden the constellation of stars—
an end to all worrisome scars.

My desirous pain you heal,
my vacuous soul your radiance daily fills.
Be the tender Baobab tree on which I lean.
Take me to your illustrious lair where passion leaps.
I will love you till the end of days.
In your embrace, I will have
my illustrious stay.

Waited in vain

You came in an angelic
       frame
Set this soul aflame
Your lipstick echoed my name
Set me on course like a game
Love you made girdled my aim
And my antelope of philandering, I maimed
In my portrait of love, you stood carved with the strings of my
sinew and veins
I kept the memory of you in me as its only celebrity of fame
I willed your personality to erect my epitaph
Even in winter
The memories of your touch like an Ivorian leaf, never withers
Now I stink like a prisoner in jail
The agony of the never-flowing water in a Santorinian pail
Separated from the romance of the seas and oceans in Niger
And their tumultuous sound during foreplay in Wales
This nimble heart pumps sick and frail
For this news of your broad laps aired by Jane

Your amorous engagements freighted in human planes
The ashes of your love shall be scattered by the sea of gross
heartache
Precipitated by your slippery strays
In the mirage of love so pure and sane
I waited all in vain

Abuse

Deeper
Sharply curved like brooding palm fronds
Her accent brawls high like raucous billows of raging wind
Her poise so proper
Pain knitted behind the soles of her feet
Life got her spines propped against the walls of gagged
expression
She sniffed her own voice, like a child petrified by her own
awesomeness
She stood on the stage of solitude and rehearsed into the void
She knelt and wept, bruised herself with the detritus of the
fallen mirror and wailed:
I am a woman. I am not the dent on manliness.
My face is not the punching bag for your sleazy knuckle dusters,
nor the flare of
your insecurities
I am a woman. Not 'woe man'. Woman!

Sepia

She veered off the rail of elegance like a cookie
cartwheeled by the flat tubes of wantonness.
         She went on and on until like a
pack of virulently shuffled cards in the numb,
numbness of the faceless night, her pomp crumbled.
She was the Duchess of my heart but the Emperor of all my
         sorrows.
Every night, she took her place beside
the shit-piled and debris-cobbled *Obalende* bridge.
Different men in flashy cars would pull over to check her inner
         light.
She would wriggle her waist and say if they paid
her well, they would enjoy her creamy pie.
She knew her body is a beautiful country,
the fad of travellers in a carnivorous city.
Her troubles began when she met Brother Jero,
they both saw the orange night-fall in Soweto.
And when she discovered the thing around her neck,
her life underwent grisly trials and metamorphosis.
She knew her salvation would not come by chance.
She sought succour from the white-garment
seers who told her about death and the
king's horsemen.

She was told to scoop salinated water from
the tongue of the ocean and that she must set forth at dawn.
She struck a stranger's pose, waiting for an angel,
her tears became her instrument for measuring time.
The circumference of her pain became half of a yellow sun,
she had begun to stink like a corpse flower in her season of
          crimson blossom.
She was buried in a litany of purple hibiscus by the children of
          blood and bones
from the anthills of the Savannah,
anchored by her lost sister, the Americanah,
whose eyes tell her stories, enshrined in the inferno of silence.
But to mourn a woman in her prime is never the joy of
          motherhood.

Festooned

She ran her shrunken fingers across the
stains on the apron of her effort.
And like a child in rare admiration of dirt's glamour,
she dipped her crumpled thumb into her
black tongue and licked the juice of grief.
She wondered why her frantic efforts at life
and enterprise never earned his emotional
comfort nor his conscientious goodwill.
His cruel winks tore the elegant drape on
the salacious curve of her virtuous intentions.
He would promise to change but his righteous
acts were always deranged, squeezing every pint
from the veins of her loving kindness.
And until now, nothing has changed except
the concrete of her love for him.
They have become the blood-clotted cornerstone of his
        epitaph.

Isle of lying mirrors

Our names beg for ancestral validation,
yet we seek the glitz of civilization from blonde names
and joggle nebulous alphabets for Western accreditation.
We prance in foreign shoes to navigate our native paths.

In the isle of lying mirrors,
we intermeddle with assorted wisdom to bear the harrowing
        grip of snow
and spite the cracked, whistling wind that hoists the flag of
        Harmattan.

In the isle of lying mirrors,
we despise the tropical mirror for not reflecting a white face on
        a dark neck.
We relish the luxury of slavery in lost lands of fantasies to the
        warmth of our native land.
Our loss will be posterity, lost in the alley of the primal
        relevance of native names.

The road

I purr past woods, lakes, fog and hearts
I fly over mountains, hills, waters and gasps
I clean lungs, bridges, tunnels and breath
I lend carousels of caution to pilgrims
Veterans and hiking troglodytes
I spin years like rolling dollars
I switch lanes with tides, dusk and the crispy gobs of sunshine
I unlock the locks of autumn
Suckle the frosty flakes of winter
Treat travellers to a circus of mirage
And tend the crimson cramps of colourful seasons
I am the length of perseverance and the screech of
        accomplishment
I am the restaurant of forlorn stations and homebound
        passengers
I am the waist of many waters and the sandy grain of
        bloodlines
I am the earthen lair of cadaverous memories
I am the slope of desolation and the steep-stair of globalisation
I bring you the hazel-box of fate or the voluptuous ribbon of
        luck
I am the tomb of haste and the womb of chance
I am the road.

I and the ants

The red ants didn't sniff my empty hands for crumbs tonight.
How could they have deserted me in this jail of lack?
The Samaritan woman in a jaded blouse
didn't let us help her out with her wares this afternoon.
She held out a mean gaze, dripping like the water of ablution
		to rinse the flesh of our ignorance from the grip of her
		frail evolution.
She wore a nose mask and left no perky grains for us today.
Her words shrunk from contagion into hurtful whispers.
Seven kettles of agony were strung to her infected lungs to
		allay her wheezing breath.
Her robust frame broke into sumptuous carcasses for worms
		and termites.
In the haze of the arrogant news of her sudden passing,
I and the ants, in this hunger-infested lockdown, under the
		pissing watch of the withering night, cried for her.

Autumn leaves

Loan your worries to the leaves in autumn
Splash your magic smiles on feeble knees
Surf on the dumb torrents of lonesome tides
Eject your feet from the suntanned skin of sinking sands
Reshuffle your rickety cards of misgivings
Hide your last card of vengeance behind the truckload of a
        judge's gavel of benevolence.

Check up on animosity with the wild grin of a jester
Douse sulphuric words with the chortles of an impervious
        drunkard
Embrace the closing dusk of renewal
Bridle the grey horse of your vainglory
Muzzle the ox that treads the grain of bitterness
Tend the succulent foliage of happiness and peace with
        candour
Throw your light far into creaks of sincere yearnings
Let no man snatch your joy.

Your fight is over

It went from grains of innocuous gossips to a catalogue of
dead faces
You became indisposed from daily immersion in the gallons of
antiseptics
You trudged with fate, the horrendous desert of safety
equipment
You escaped the land mines of infected bodies and shut out
the pathetic chortles of excited economic cannibals
seated on the pyramid of dead bodies
The political serpents bit harder on the starving wit of the
vulnerable with the venom of mischief
Dumping crumbs of palliatives to mock the crucibles of
hungry masses
You snorted at the magnanimous leash of transatlantic greed
and acephalous policies
You ratted out the holes in all sanctimonious, propaganda-
sanctioned, economic boars
You cringe at every slippery hold on the waistline of time

And like the sunflower, the sun beckoned
your last breath to bloom

Your turgid wrinkles were like the gossamer lines on a sallow
map
Your hasty dawn looked forward to long dusk as your world
spilt away
You looked gristly as you were lowered into the river of
darkness
Now your fight is over
May the lights guide you home.

The Jobberman

The skies had a fallen countenance today.
The bread-bickering bird got entangled in the crushing snare
            of the
crooked fowler.

This French hen did not come home to roost today,
his blood-stained boots were the black box of his incinerated
        body.

They said his cannon scalp first flew like a cowardly
knight in a feast of war
before the raging clubs split his skull into a pair of melons.

His rheumy eyes bled for mercy before his
tongue was harvested with their patina knife.

The culling birds didn't chirp when the sun nestled behind the
            clouds.
They fooled him with the camaraderie of a warm welcome.
They knew he was a gluttonous political jobberman
before they brought the cruise of his economic loot to a fatal
        halt.

The large sum of money in his green bag was
carted away by the reckless mobs.
The news said the powerful man had some
of the stimulus package in his coffers before
he was lost to the cold hands of death.
The mobs claimed the economic power of their
lives had been long lost to the reins of vile
mercantilism and they lost loved ones to the
monstrous pandemic, COVID-19, too.
No peace for the wicked was their vociferous chant.
The homeless wind cradled his moist ashes into lonesome
		bollocks.
Death jostles the gavel of equity was his favorite quote.

To Port Harcourt

Marco Polo tyres swallowing the asphalt to Port Harcourt
in the belly of the impetuous road.
I witness the croaking clouds dart at the silver moon for
         dinner,
past the haunted mien of the Niger bridge and
the desolate plains of Onitsha market.
Amidst the cranks of broken shafts and
the recurring hydrogenation of the ailing carburettor,
the morgue exhaled water to the living.
Cadavers lobbed kindness to fagged-out ashes.
Our weary eyes burst open from the sharp cuts of translucent
         fog lights.
We cringed at the sight of prowling ritualists
and corrupt policemen
camouflaged as flower dressers and enforcing
state laws by extortion at the bypass of Benin-Ore Road.
Clouds of hope garrisoned our hearts from
the recitals of contrite hymns.
The dumb bus drivers-cum-mechanics coupled
the skeleton of the ratchet bus back to life.
Alas! Blessed are you when your driver is a
metallic sorcerer of a frustrating order.

I met nightfall

I met nightfall
in a huge, dusty hall.

She has eyes as owls and grins of moonlight.
She whispered darkness and limped on limbs marked with
        scaly webs.
She reeks of sour oil and recurrent mares,
brimming with hailstones and fire
reposed in the womb of Hades.
She leaned on broken tripods of bad luck,
wild seduction and brokenness for simpletons.
She is the despicable taskmaster at the valley of the shadows of
        death.
She melts away like frost at the wake of redemptive dawn.

I met nightfall,
I bent her crusty wings and the tree of courage within me grew
        tall.
I tore the jagged jaw of fear and despised the guts of wild
        beasts of encumbrances
as I trudged the forest of the shadows of mares.

Stay alive

shun the life of rebels
lest your fate becomes like the devil's
with feet bound to hell's gate.

shun violence,
it blots out your memory of kindness
and deeds of goodness.

shun intents of trouble,
your vanity it doubles
and your soul it smashes to rubble.

shun revenge,
it multiplies your rags of regret.

shun abnormal diet,
it dulls your physique
and intellectual quotient.

shun parasitic friends,
they cast your soul into fiendish nets.

shun indecision,
it may grant you speed without direction.

shun sinful pets,
they caress your soul with stings of death.

shun strife,
it profits not a dime.

shun randy acts,
they spread your illicit desires in the air like kites
and plunge your light into an illimitable void.

The smell of gratitude

Head the running clouds
Beat the rain into a steel spear
Crowd us out with the petrichor of bliss
Pierce us with moist and freshness
Curve the sunrays into a bow
Bless our frost and folding palms with warmth
Rearrange with nostalgia the dust-rife shelves of memory
Teach us the smell of gratitude
Sport our teeth with the cookie jar of new names
Let the lumberman of mirth fell the luscious tree of our
        execrable burdens
Let the riverine palms of time, for each day, wrap us in the
        swaddling clothes of joy.

Fela

High priest of the redeemable vulnerables in the Kalakuta
        republic
The tambourine of grit in the besieged orchestra of democracy
The maverick of the Afrobeat dynasty and the dreaded song
        on the sallow lips of zombies
Voice as wide as a mother's crossed arms
Purveyor of the electrocuting Konga instrumentation for
        political dimwits
Back ripped with batons and blatant wounds as testaments to
        the struggle to pluck Logs of myopia from the sagged
        eyes of economic simpletons
A thorn in the flesh of religious mongrels and faith mongers
The anaesthetic serum of conscientious journalists
Sore pain in the butt of the ruler
The gallstone in the kidney of corrupt souls
A transcontinental cocktail of vermin for greedy
Politicians suffering the mental illness of power perpetuity
Fela, the decent descent of status quo bender
        Abami Eda
        Jagunlabi
        A venerable statesman
The fearless savant of a new world order

I CAN'T BREATHE

For GEORGE FLOYD murdered on purpose by Derrick Chauvin, a Minneapolis cop, on the 25th of May, 2020.

You knelt on my neck
My hands cuffed behind my back
You clipped my head to the floor till my life peeled away
My plea, a grinning sport for your devious cult
My agony, a star of honour to your badge of racism
I can't breathe

Ghoul

His hands, like the creepy fangs of a ghoul
ate through my quivering thighs,
pushing past my objections, tears, sore and silence
and left my bloody, shrunken self in a catatonic blob.
And daily, I await his carcass, cremated in a running bathtub.

▌I remember you

You are the contour of Mississippi,
The texture of chance,
A lonely, running road.

You are the chalice of double consciousness,
The slurp of a backstroking meadow,
The calculus of rejection and the blur of reasoning.

You are the curve of vicarious interplanetary cravings,
The crack of discipline,
The cumulonimbus of dissonance and the sledge of nostalgia.

You are the angst of disuse,
The cathedral of empathy,
Flailing noose of misogyny and the defiant shadow that stalks
          sunrise.

You are the potluck of fog,
The balustrade of subterfuge and the soulmate of charm.
You are honey, pouring slowly into the wilderness of time.

Ashes, laterites, and termites

In loving memory of Segun Oloyede, my Dad indeed

A song drowns in my throat as the moon in silvery dusts
A verse gropes the thistles of my tongue as night in darkness
I yawn like a crow on rubble as I sit on the sycamore of loss
I wrung the lyre of grief for your demise from the withering
        arms of a Jacaranda
I hashed the rhythm of sorrow from the burning tulips of your
        memory
My voice falls like the evening tide as I found a cleft in silence
        by your epitaph
From dust you came and to dust you have returned
Let the ashes, laterites and termites lug you to Zion.
Adieu, Papa.

The back of Africa

Every night we sit like kegs of ornaments around the market
        square.
Our warriors fight for pride and honour,
        legs adorned with braces jingle the chorus of freedom,
history visibly scarified on our cheeks and imprinted
in the doggedness of our spirit,
        the back of Africa can never be put out to the ground.
        Like dust, we rise and furnish our hope with grit.
Our ears glean the rhythmic pout of the Atlantic
Ocean and tingle at the novel tales of our economic
        fortification.
We mould herbs, Iroko, and dust into riches
and forge vast and gigantic industries from seashells and
        cowries.
Our colour, deep as the black panther's, conquers
the stroking anguish of slavery and colonialism.
We clap and dance to the invigorating
percussions of *omele* and *sekere* on Kilimanjaro.
We rinse the stains of bitterness in Lake Victoria
and dance the dance of deliverance from the
fetters of yesteryears on Olumo rock,
replacing artefacts of woe with the sweet-scented bouquet of a
        new dawn.

▎BODMAS of grief

(for all the persons captured by insurgents)

To bracket a village with bazookas, machetes and loathsome
      columns of rapists,
divide members of sinless infants and aged lots in their sleep,
mangle the neck of the leaders of tomorrow and
ground them to dust with tractors of gruesomeness.

Wreck the peace of a generation with the shrapnel of
      corruption,
seize the unsoiled maidens to settle the scores of
religious beliefs and satisfy your thirst for bed-creaking sports.

Detonate amongst innocent daily bread seekers,
the ruthless bombs of the seven virgin-seeking bigots.

Bury in the garb of nepotism, **the gory apparatus** of
political-cum-ethnic distortions and defiant
plots of sad Sarduanas, cassock-touting sophomaniacs.

Underplay the blinded wrath of these
indoctrinated cretins forged into abduction syndicate,
cowering in the blood-flooded Sambisa forest,
feasting on the tears and blood of the innocent.

These callous wimps of terror, like ravenous beasts
devouring to desolated stupor,
the sweet game of our corporate inheritance,
with politicking avarice, is the BODMAS of grief.

Sacrament of bullets

*(for all the lives lost at the Lekki toll gate during the #endsars
protest on 20th of October, 2020)*

May you trouble your assailants and give them no peace.
They might have washed your blood from the floor
but not from their hands.
Justice must be served.

We all were gathered here like brazen clouds
at the toll gate of servitude,
garrisoned by the wind of engorging strength,
billowing the threads of our sincere concerns,
raising sweat-stained placards of our civil rights
and bearing scorched cardboard of our democratic demands
to end the impunity of police brutality with our raindrop of
        pleas
before the troops of cowardice came like
ravens to gorge out the bowels of our bravery.

They dug their fangs of terror into the neck
of our resolve with the fireworks of assailants.
Our voices were drowning in the torrent of shells with no
        tribal marks,
our blood became the toll-fare to enforce a
new order for the coming generation,
our tears and bruises, a fresh delicacy for
these callous economic maggots and political vermin.
Let this be the testament that we did not break
when we knelt, rounded up by the blazing rifles of zombies
at the behest of political wolves;

that we interrogated the value of our freedom,
chanting our national anthem and reaffirming our pledge,
and raised our flag as the palliative for peace;

that we made a mockery of death and nipped fear in our
        pouch.
That at this solemn altar of peaceful protests,
our bodies were desecrated with the sacrament of bullets.

SARS

(Sacrilegious, Anti-Reasoning Squad)

Shameless, gun-totting coven of brigands
Faux security unit of abduction and debauchery
Retail store of body parts and harvested organs
Ruthless syndicate of terror and mass pauperization
Allies of traffickers and daylight hijackers
Peddlers of variant victims' confiscated possessions
Stooge of ritualists and glamorous hoodlums
Horde of bloodthirsty miscreants
Circle of vengeful, vicious and demented ex-convicts
Mercenaries of sorrow, tears and blood

SARS!

Smother and torture your victims till they
confess to unsubstantiated accusations
Arrest without cause and documentation and
detain in desolated stations or decrepit hideouts

Repel any attempt for legal representation to
prove the victims' innocence without paying a fat ransom

Shed enough blood and brag of no consequence
SARS, the Dunkirk of atrocious stock in trade of brutality
Mass murder and impunity, under the auspices of
gaslighting state machineries

May the roads bring you luck

Ale for your thirsty throat
Oil for your blistering feet
Air for your wheezing lungs
Humor for your heavy cheeks
Balm for your sore thumb
Cheque of love for your insolvent heart
Compass for your wandering dreams
May the roads bring you luck.

In the memory of memory

I sat on the wobbling stool of vainglory
Cast my crooked gaze on the falling stars of orient disharmony
Ate a dozen *kolanuts* to the savoury reminiscence of past
      glories
Talked in the theatrical verve of 'Giringori', a quintessence of
      comedy
And revved to the paeon of Zebudayah
A man drew thick lines of timbre across the hearts of men in
      his time
      Halleluya!

In the memory of memory lives the mute tellers of homeless
      stories
Handless drummers drumming life into broken spirits and
      wretched limbs

In the memory of memory
Painters painted paintings that walked
Out of the paintings to paint the exact painting of the painter's
      painting
The whistler's whistle whistled the whistling the whistler's
      whistle should have
whistled
Shadows squash substance as memory revers destiny
They shook at arm's length
And walked past the cemetery of good intentions
Laying wreaths, oars and lantern by the shores of
Vagrant dreams and noble memories

BIO

Oloyede Michael Taiwo is a poet, storyteller, copywriter, scriptwriter, screenwriter, spoken-word artiste, playwright, producer and philomath.

He has appeared on different TV and radio stations, propagating the gospel according to poetry and holding conferences on politics and economic issues.

He wrote and produced the play, "Wrinkles, dimples, naira and bets," during the Lagos Theatre Festival, 2020, in partnership with the British Council.

He has performed in several literary events and one of the largest gospel concerts in Lagos—Cross Concert.

He curates diverse didactic and literary events, such as: Learning With Celebrities Conference, Lagos Poetrython, Fireflies & Bumblebees and the Lagos Poetrython Spoken Word Academy.

He has been shortlisted for the Etisalat Flash Fiction Prize and long listed for the Quramo Writers' Prize for literature. He loves psychedelic music and the riff of bass guitar strings. He is an associate of the Academy of Modern Applied Psychology and also an associate of Financial Freedom Academy, a financial solution organisation based in the U.K. He is also a transmedia content architect, product developer, integrated brand marketer and a certified finance and investment analyst.

Taiwo loves to meditate and enjoy the tranquillity of wandering in a liminal orifice.

AUTHOR'S NOTE

Thank you for the time you have taken to read this book. I hope you enjoyed the poems in it.

If you loved the book and have a minute to spare, I would appreciate a short review on the page or site where you bought it. I greatly appreciate your help in promoting my work. Reviews from readers like you make a huge difference in helping new readers choose the book.

Thank you!

Oloyede Michael Taiwo

www.ingramcontent.com/pod-product-compliance
Lightning Source LLC
Chambersburg PA
CBHW031356060726
47590CB00007B/2811